23 Wall Street

Copyright © 1964 by Morgan Guaranty Trust Company of New York

Wall Street is a community where past mingles easily with present and future. Early history of city, state, and nation is everywhere in the area, for this was the original New York—a seat of governments before it became the center of finance. At home amid tradition, Wall Street lives respectfully but comfortably with its long heritage. It finds the backdrop of yesterday a congenial setting for doing today's work and making tomorrow's plans.

In this setting thrives a unique concentration of human skills and talents. They are occupied in diverse ways, but their common concern is with the workings of money in an economy that runs on money. The skills and talents belong to central bankers, commercial bankers, investment bankers, stockbrokers, dealers in all kinds of securities and commodities, insurance underwriters, managers of funds, lawyers, economists, and providers of a host of other specialized services. The gathering of these human resources in a compact and cohesive community, no two parts of which are more than a short walk apart, helps give Wall Street its distinctive character and its distinctive usefulness to the nation and the world.

Besides being a community, Wall Street is a street. It cuts straight from Trinity Church on lower Broadway to the East River, a little more than one-third of a mile, and for most of that length is a narrow corridor between tall buildings. Here and there, however, the shade of towering skyscrapers is broken by a sudden opening of light and air. Such a place is the intersection where Wall meets Broad Street. There stand two buildings incongruously low amid their surroundings. One, a colonnaded temple exemplary of the Greek Revival in American architecture, is the Federal Hall Memorial, a national shrine on the site where George Washington was inaugurated. From its steps, John Ward's bronze of the first President looks across the street toward a marble house of clean, classical line relieved by details in the style of the Italian Renaissance. This is 23 Wall Street. An address prominent in finance for nearly a century, it is now—in combination with an adjoining 38-story tower—the main office of Morgan Guaranty Trust Company of New York.

Installation of the bank's headquarters here, early in 1964, came amid a cluster of anniversaries: 50 years since the original completion of the 23 Wall building as the home of J. P. Morgan & Co.; 100 years since the founding of

In the door of 23 Wall, a reflection of the scene across the street: Federal Hall Memorial and the statue of George Washington, on the site where the first President was inaugurated in 1789.

23

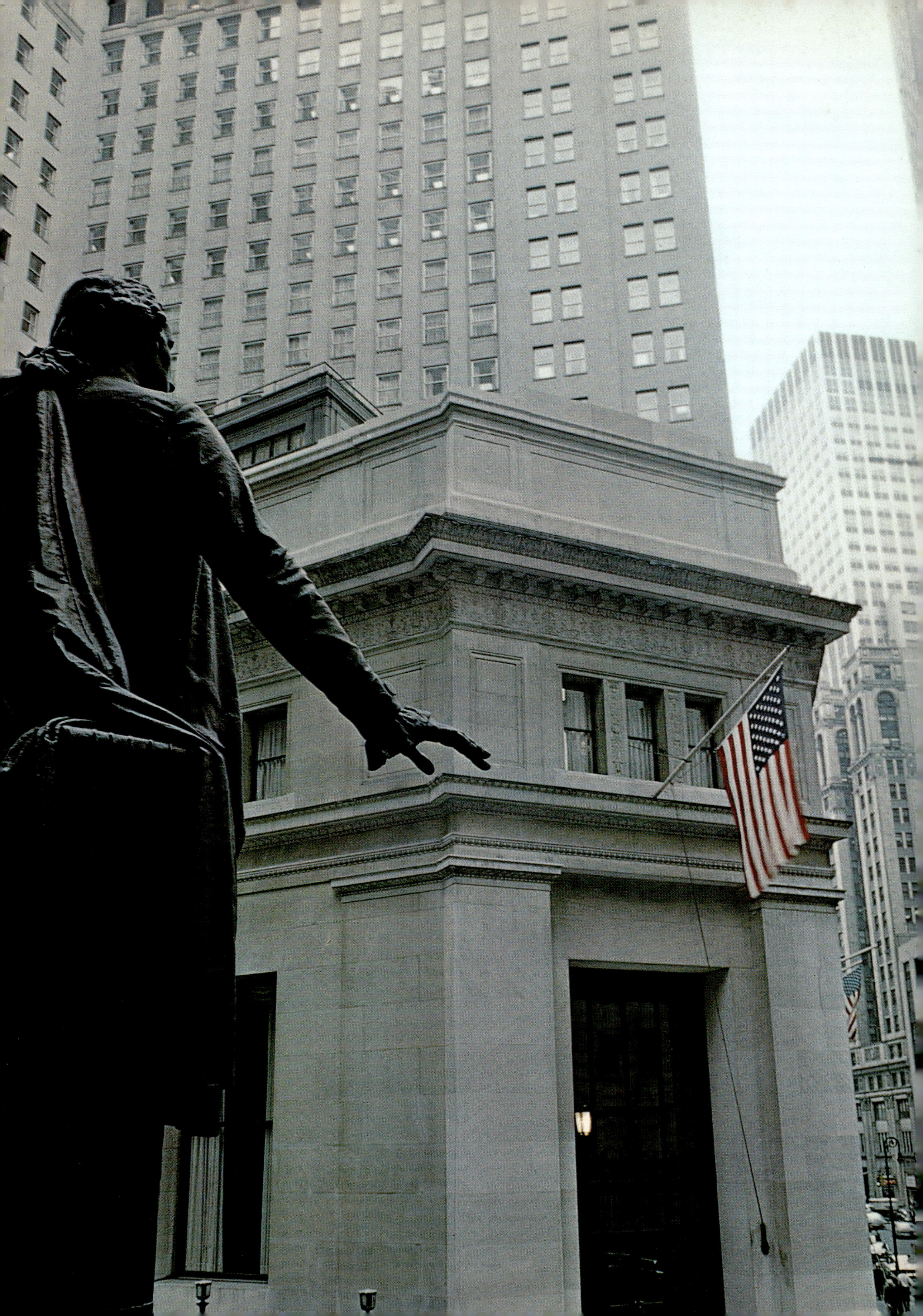

This building preceded the present one at 23 Wall. It was the home of Drexel Morgan & Co.

On Wall Street at the corner of Broad, No. 23 and the tall building that rises behind it form Morgan Guaranty's main office. Outside, the corner building is as it was when it went up in 1914. Inside there have been changes.

Guaranty Trust Company of New York, which merged with the Morgan bank in 1959 to form Morgan Guaranty; 125 years since the birth of the present institution's earliest predecessor, Bank of Commerce in New York.

Each of these enterprises had its start within hailing distance of the present center of Morgan Guaranty's worldwide operations. The beginnings of J. P. Morgan & Co. trace to a one-room office at 54 Exchange Place, opposite the 15 Broad Street building that now forms the high-rise portion of Morgan Guaranty's headquarters. There, about 1860 (there is no reliable record of the exact date), J. Pierpont Morgan went into business dealing in bills of exchange drawn on England. Later he moved across the street to 53 Exchange Place. In 1871 he joined forces with Drexel & Co., an established Philadelphia firm which wished to strengthen its position in New York. Together they formed Drexel Morgan & Co. The new firm put up its own building, completed in 1873, at Wall and Broad Streets, on the corner where Morgan Guaranty's main office now stands. Drexel Morgan was succeeded by J. P. Morgan & Co. in 1895.

Bank of Commerce, organized in 1839 and subsequently renamed National Bank of Commerce, had its first place of business in a basement at 46 Wall, just a block east of No. 23. Guaranty Trust's predecessor, called New York Guaranty and Indemnity Company, started life at 14 Broad Street. Much later, in 1929, Commerce and Guaranty were to merge. Ties of origin thus link Morgan Guaranty to the corner at the hub of New York's financial district. But history of a deeper kind also swirls about this crossroads.

A CORNER OF HISTORY

In 1700, New York's second City Hall was built where the Federal Hall Memorial now stands. It housed both city and colonial governments. By that time, the timber wall from which the street takes its name was already gone—victim of rot and of foragers for firewood. It had been put up by the Dutch in 1653 to shut out marauding Indians and British, but the latter had foiled its purpose by capturing the city with an attack by sea in 1664.

The Hall was the scene in 1735 of John Peter Zenger's trial and acquittal on charges of seditious libel brought by government officials whom he had criticized in his newspaper. The Stamp Act Congress, which hardened colonial resistance to British rule, met there in 1765. The Continental Congress used the Hall beginning in 1785. Renamed Federal Hall, it was enlarged and remodeled to house the Congress of 1789, the first convened under the Constitution. Among that body's achievements was passage of the Bill of Rights. The entire Federal government was quartered in the building from Washington's inauguration in April 1789 until August of the following year.

Across the street, on the site that was to become 23 Wall, the events of colonial times were less momentous. Still they form a revealing part of the city's narrative. The earliest recorded owner of land on the southeast corner was Elizabeth Drisius, who used it as an orchard about the middle of the 17th century. She sold two lots in 1682, one to a laborer for $25 and the other to a bricklayer for $30. By 1700 some of the land had come into the hands of the city, which built its police station, called the "watch house," on the corner. Pillory, stocks, cage, and whipping post were outside in the yard to afford public display of the more painful kinds of punishment imposed on offenders.

Later in the 18th century, Alexander Hamilton's home was at 33 Wall Street, just east of the watch house. He had his law office several doors down the street at 57 Wall. Elizabeth Bayley Seton, with her husband, lived at 27 Wall from 1794 to 1798. After her husband's death, she founded an order of Roman Catholic nuns; as Mother Seton, she has been proposed for canonization.

Commerce and finance began to gain a foothold around the corner of Wall and Broad Streets about the end of the 18th century. A group of merchants dealing in the debt securities of the new Federal government formed an exchange in 1792, under a buttonwood tree on Wall Street near William Street. Since the government bonds of those days were called stock, the merchants called their organiza-

A chandelier in the style of the Louis XV period lights the main banking room. The fixture, 16 feet tall, hangs from a ceiling that is 35 feet high.

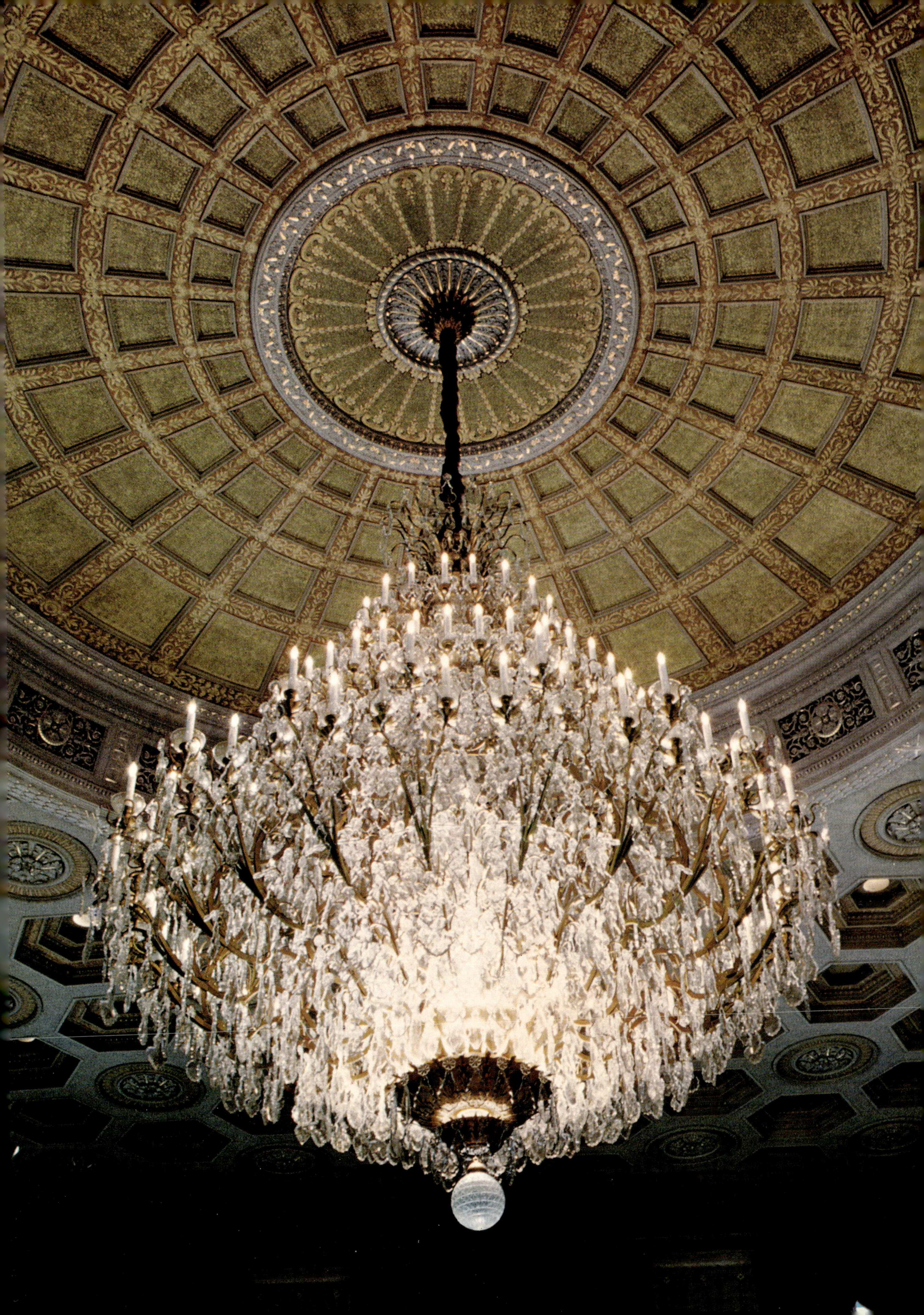

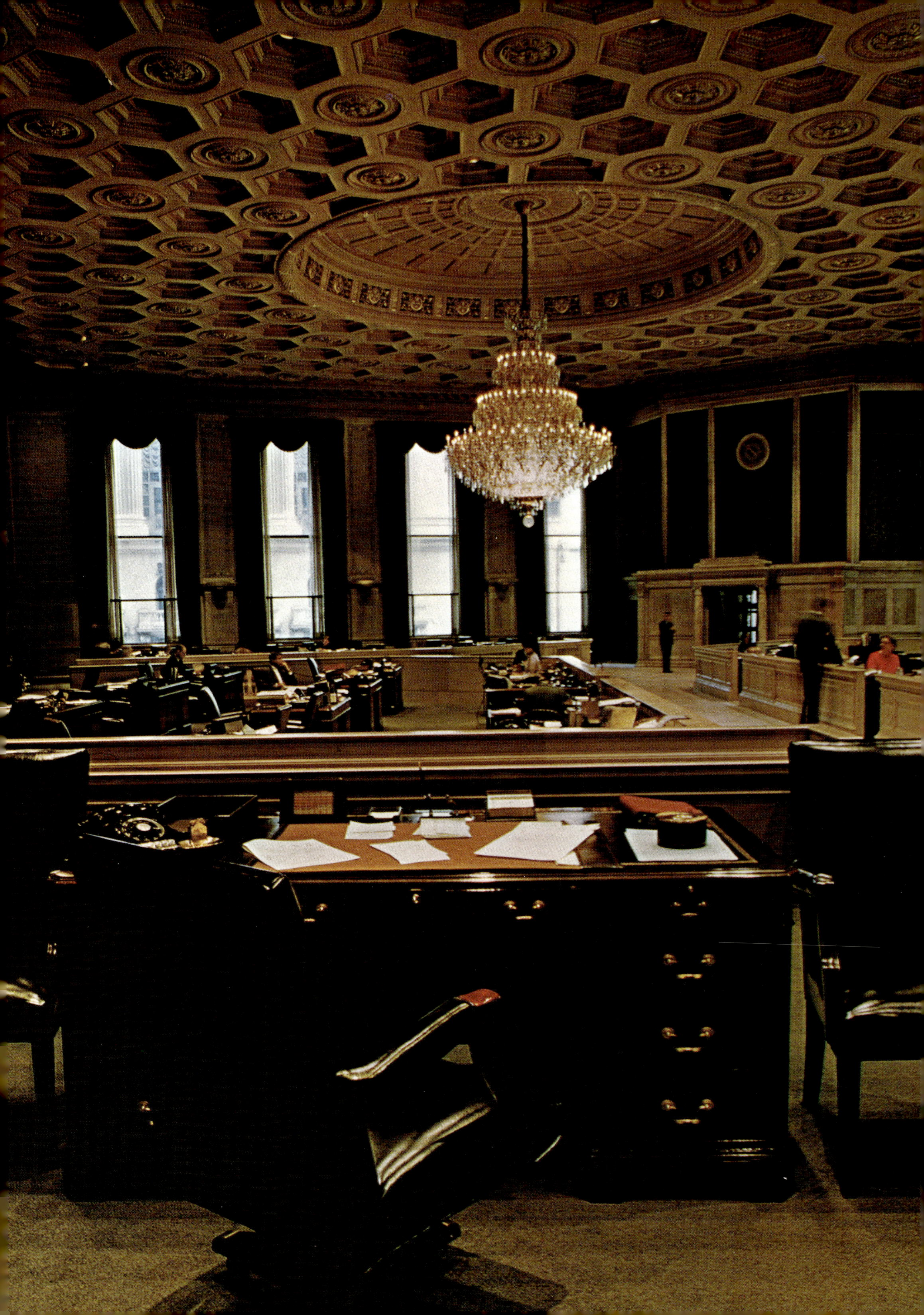

tion a stock exchange. Their code of rules was the formal beginning of the New York Stock Exchange, which has its present home on the southwest corner of Wall and Broad.

Gradually, offices crowded out residences in the Wall Street area. The transition was pushed by the rebuilding that occurred after a disastrous fire that swept lower Manhattan in 1835. A row of narrow buildings on the land now occupied by Morgan Guaranty had such tenants in the 1850's as brokers, lawyers, architects, commission merchants, auctioneers, three telegraph companies, a banknote engraver, an insurance firm, a printer, and two coal companies. A stand at the curb offered raw oysters.

BANK OF COMMERCE

This view shows a portion of the main banking floor, looking toward windows on the Broad Street side.

With the growth of industry and trade throughout the young country came greater need for financial services. Meanwhile, a series of developments in the latter 1830's had an important bearing on the evolution of a banking system in America. The second Bank of the United States, which during the two decades of its life acted as both central bank and commercial bank, lost its Federal charter in 1836. The bank's headquarters were in Philadelphia; when it went into eclipse, New York's place as the nation's financial center was confirmed.

Also, the end of Federally sponsored banking withdrew the government from direct participation in the field of private finance, opening broader opportunities for the state-chartered banks. There were nearly 600 of these in the land. The panic of 1837 induced an epidemic of failures, but scarcely slowed the rate at which new banks were being formed. The opening of new institutions received further impetus with the enactment of "free-banking" laws in some states, notably in New York in 1839. Under these laws, the designated state official could grant a bank charter to any party meeting certain stated conditions; before, each charter had required a special act of the state legislature.

This was the setting for the establishment, early in 1839, of Bank of Commerce in New York, the first bank among those that eventually would be succeeded by the present Morgan Guaranty Trust Company. The sponsors included some of the principal New York financiers, who looked to the new bank in part to take over the stabilizing role which had been one of the functions of the Bank of the United States. To that end, Commerce was from the outset a sizable institution in the context of its times. The initially subscribed capital was $5 million. The first loan the new bank agreed to make, even before it had formally begun operation, was an advance of half a million dollars to New York State to widen and deepen the Erie Canal.

Bank of Commerce's main business was lending to commercial and industrial customers, but it also was a mainstay of the Federal government, repeatedly mobilizing funds to tide the Treasury over credit crises. When Congress established the national banking system during the Civil War, it was so anxious to have Bank of Commerce join that it amended the National Bank Act to resolve a conflict with Commerce's articles of association. Urging the amendment, Representative Samuel Hooper of Massachusetts said of the bank: "It has done more to sustain the Government since the Rebellion commenced than any other bank." With the legal obstacle cleared, the bank entered the national system in 1865 and changed its name to National Bank of Commerce.

In the meantime, its growth had necessitated a series of changes in location. It moved in 1842 to 32 Wall Street, alongside the site of Federal Hall. That historic structure had been torn down in 1812; a makeshift building for use of the Customs Service stood in its place for a couple of decades, and then the present building with its classic columned façade was erected as the permanent Custom House. It served that purpose from 1842 until 1862, when it became the Subtreasury. From 1920 to 1924 it was the home of the Federal Reserve Bank of New York. Now it is the Federal Hall National Memorial.

Bank of Commerce stayed at 32 Wall until 1854, then spent a few years in rented quarters at Broad Street and Exchange Place, and in 1857 moved to a permanent home at the northwest corner of Nassau and Cedar Streets. From that location, some 70 years later, it would merge with the

A portrait of J. Pierpont Morgan painted by Baca-Flor in 1911 is on the south wall of the main banking room. It is reproduced in full at the top of this page.

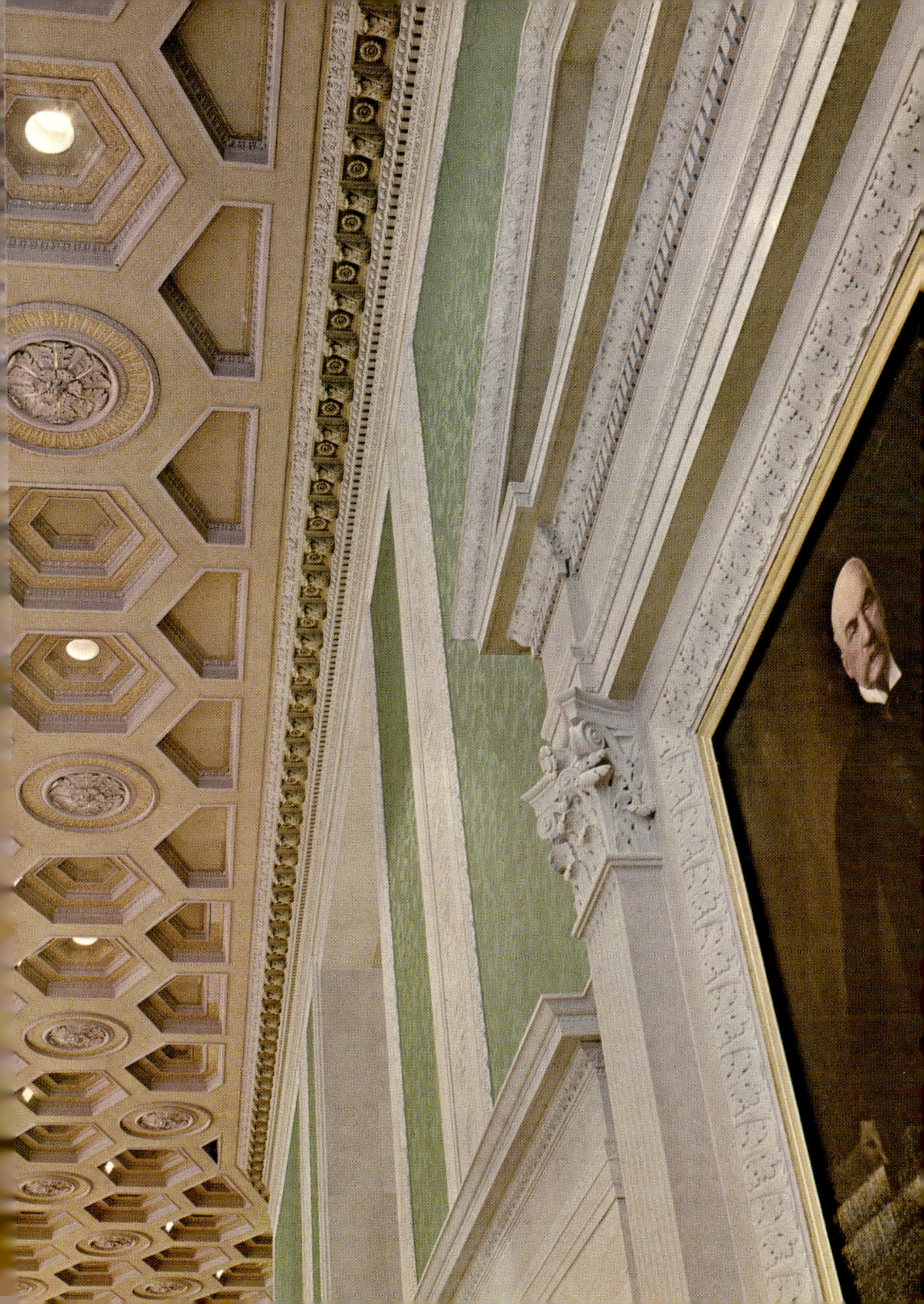

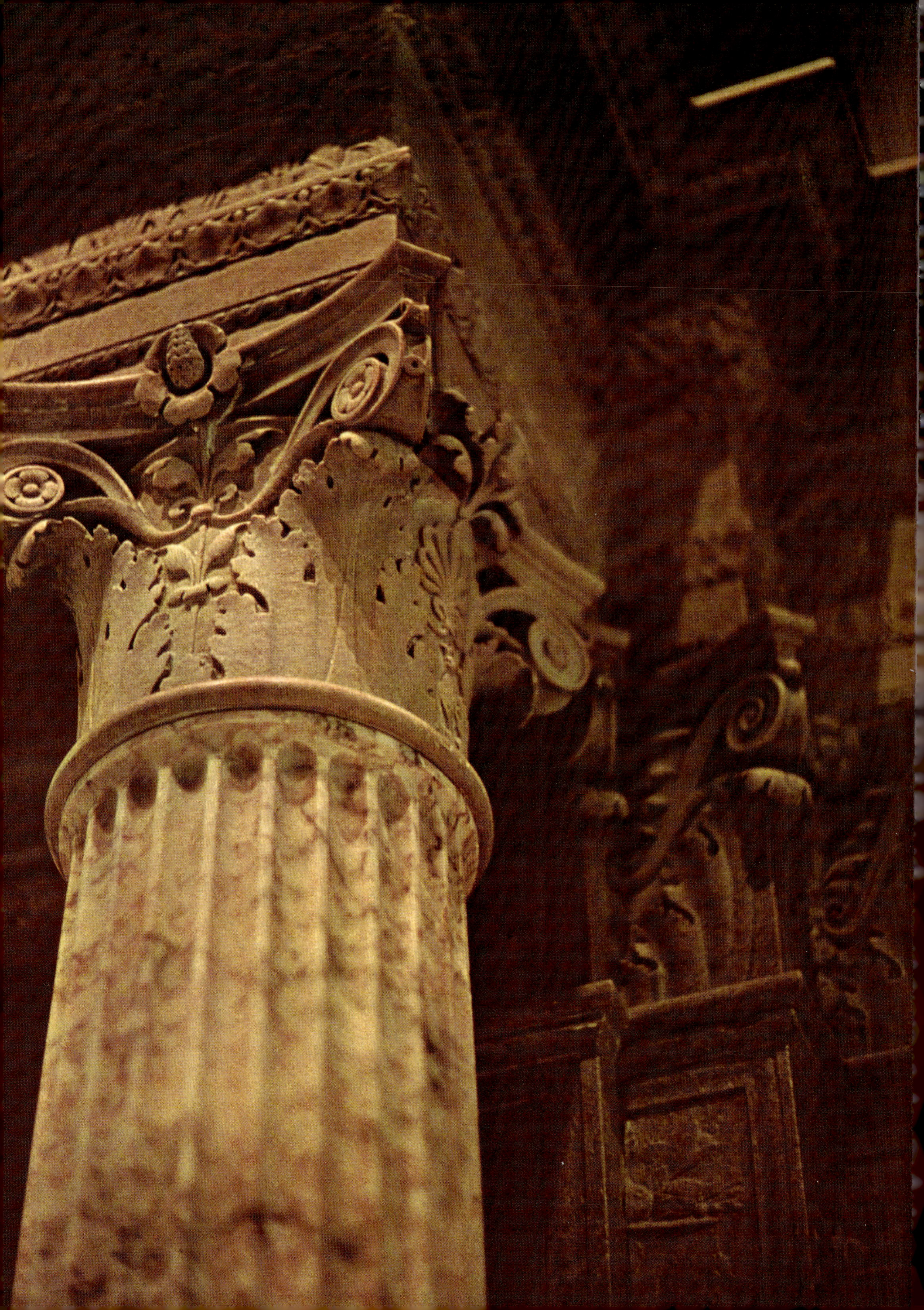

Four Corinthian columns of marble have been retained from the original interior. Shown is one of a pair framing the main entrance.

younger Guaranty Trust Company of New York, which by then had become a near neighbor, located at 140 Broadway.

For several years after its founding in 1864 as New York Guaranty and Indemnity Company, Guaranty's business was mainly lending against warehouse receipts, a field of financing previously not much explored by banks. The initial capital of $100,000 was increased in 1865 to $2 million, but subsequently a period of retrenchment set in and for a while there was thought of liquidating the company. In 1891, however, a group representing the Mutual Life Insurance Company led a reorganization that turned Guaranty in a new direction and launched it on a career of rapid growth. As part of the change, the bank in 1896 took a new name—Guaranty Trust Company of New York.

SIMILARITIES AND DIFFERENCES

By the time Guaranty and J. P. Morgan & Co. merged in 1959, the two institutions had come—by different paths—to fill quite similar roles in the evolving world of finance. Both had concentrated their efforts in the field that has become known as "wholesale" banking—meeting the specialized financial needs of business concerns, other banks, institutions, and individuals of substantial means. Both had won strong reputations in investment banking as well as commercial banking before the Banking Act of 1933 required separation of the two kinds of activity. Both had built a large volume of business in the growing fields of managing other people's money as trustee and giving professional advice on investments. And both had moved early and prominently into international finance.

From the start the Morgan firm had an international orientation. Pierpont Morgan's small office in the 1860's benefited from connections with the London firm which his father, Junius Spencer Morgan, had gone over from Boston to join. Originally founded in his own name by another American, George Peabody, the London house of J. S. Morgan & Co. was a forerunner of today's British merchant banking firm, Morgan Grenfell & Co. Ltd., with which Morgan Guaranty works closely in the international field. From early days, the Morgan firm in New York also had an affiliate in Paris—Drexel Harjes & Co., established in 1868 and succeeded in 1895 by Morgan Harjes & Co.

GOLD AND STEEL

The rise of the Morgan name in American finance came originally through Pierpont's success in raising capital for American companies, especially railroads, by selling their securities abroad. Having induced people to invest in these enterprises from afar, he assumed a measure of responsibility for the conduct of the ventures. Soon he was intervening in situations where railroads were in financial trouble, often because of cut-throat competition resulting from excessive

13

duplication of lines. He and his associates planned and carried out reorganizations affecting half a dozen of the major rail systems.

Around the turn of the century, a series of events of high drama thrust the firm into world-wide prominence. In 1895, it stopped a run on the nation's gold supply by forming a syndicate to raise some $65 million in gold for the Treasury by selling an issue of U. S. government bonds, half of them in Europe. Mr. Morgan assured President Cleveland that Europeans would not draw gold back from the U. S. while the bonds were being placed. It was this commitment, which the firm could confidently make because of the standing it had earned with foreign financiers, that clinched the success of the operation.

In 1901, the firm underwrote the integration of a vast complex of individual companies into the United States Steel Corporation. In a country just becoming aware of its own dimensions, the bold scope of this project caught the spark of public imagination. Many regarded as fantastic the nearly $1½-billion capitalization that was placed on the new company, but it was financed successfully by the syndicate which the Morgan firm organized and managed.

With such achievements came a role of responsibility and leadership in the Wall Street community. A few years later, during the money panic of 1907, that leadership was to face its most difficult test. Failure of a few banks in October of that year brought runs on several others. Out-of-town banks began to withdraw the funds they kept on reserve deposit in New York. The growing tightness of credit forced a number of brokerage houses to suspend operations, and at one point officials of the Stock Exchange thought it would have to close down. With confidence collapsing everywhere, there was a mad scramble to turn paper assets—such as bank deposits and securities—into cash.

The swelling demand for liquid funds was endangering institutions that were basically sound. In those days there was no central bank to mobilize resources and channel them to the points where they were temporarily needed. This void Pierpont Morgan proceeded to fill. His own firm, dealing mainly with large companies whose confidence was not easily shaken, was not directly threatened by the spreading mood of panic. But no one else was taking charge, and he thought he knew what to do. In meeting after meeting, often long into the night and against stubborn resistance, he won the agreement of the chief New York banks to put up funds to tide over those in trouble. For two weeks he held the group together, until public confidence in the banks was restored.

A pattern of success in large affairs gave Pierpont Morgan and the partners who worked with him a stature and influence far beyond the actual dollar wealth held or con-

This photograph was taken at the first meeting of Morgan Guaranty's directors held in the board room on the second floor of 23 Wall. Clockwise, from left foreground:

GEORGE S. YOUNG
*Chairman, Executive Committee
The Columbia Gas System, Inc.*

M. J. RATHBONE
*Chairman of the Board
Standard Oil Company (New Jersey)*

THOMAS S. GATES
*President
Morgan Guaranty Trust Company*

WILLIAM C. BOLENIUS
*Retired Vice Chairman of the Board
American Telephone
and Telegraph Company*

DALE E. SHARP
*Vice Chairman of the Board
Morgan Guaranty Trust Company*

JOHN T. DORRANCE, JR.
*Chairman of the Board
Campbell Soup Company*

J. PAUL AUSTIN
*President
The Coca-Cola Company*

PAUL C. CABOT
*Chairman of the Board
State Street Investment Corporation*

LONGSTREET HINTON
*Executive Vice President
Morgan Guaranty Trust Company*

THOMAS L. PERKINS
*Chairman of the Trustees
The Duke Endowment*

CARL J. GILBERT
*Chairman of the Board
The Gillette Company*

CARTER L. BURGESS
*Chairman of the Board
American Machine & Foundry Company*

JAMES M. SYMES
*Chairman, Executive Committee
The Pennsylvania Railroad Company*

HENRY C. ALEXANDER
*Chairman of the Board
Morgan Guaranty Trust Company*

CRAWFORD H. GREENEWALT
*Chairman of the Board
E. I. du Pont de Nemours & Company*

R. MANNING BROWN, JR.
*Executive Vice President
New York Life Insurance Company*

ROBERT D. MURPHY
*Director, Corning Glass Works, and
President, Corning Glass International*

HENRY S. WINGATE
*Chairman of the Board
The International Nickel Company
of Canada, Limited*

Unable to attend the meeting were:

STEPHEN D. BECHTEL
*Chairman of the Board
Bechtel Corporation*

DONALD P. KIRCHER
*President
The Singer Company*

THOMAS S. LAMONT

L. F. MC COLLUM
*Chairman of the Board
Continental Oil Company*

JOHN M. MEYER, JR.
*Executive Vice President
Morgan Guaranty Trust Company*

HOWARD J. MORGENS
*President
The Procter & Gamble Company*

ROBERT T. STEVENS
*President
J. P. Stevens & Co., Inc.*

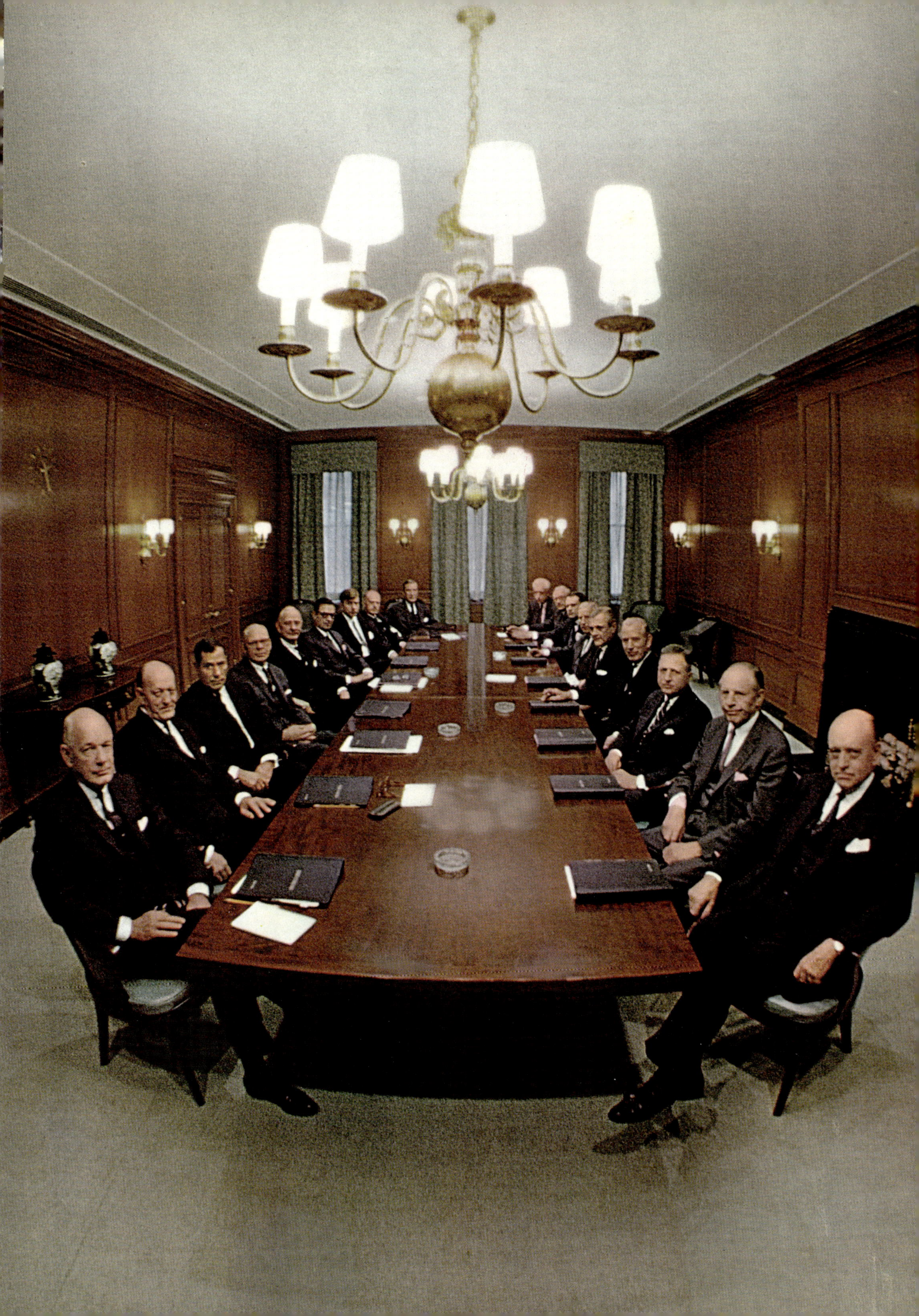

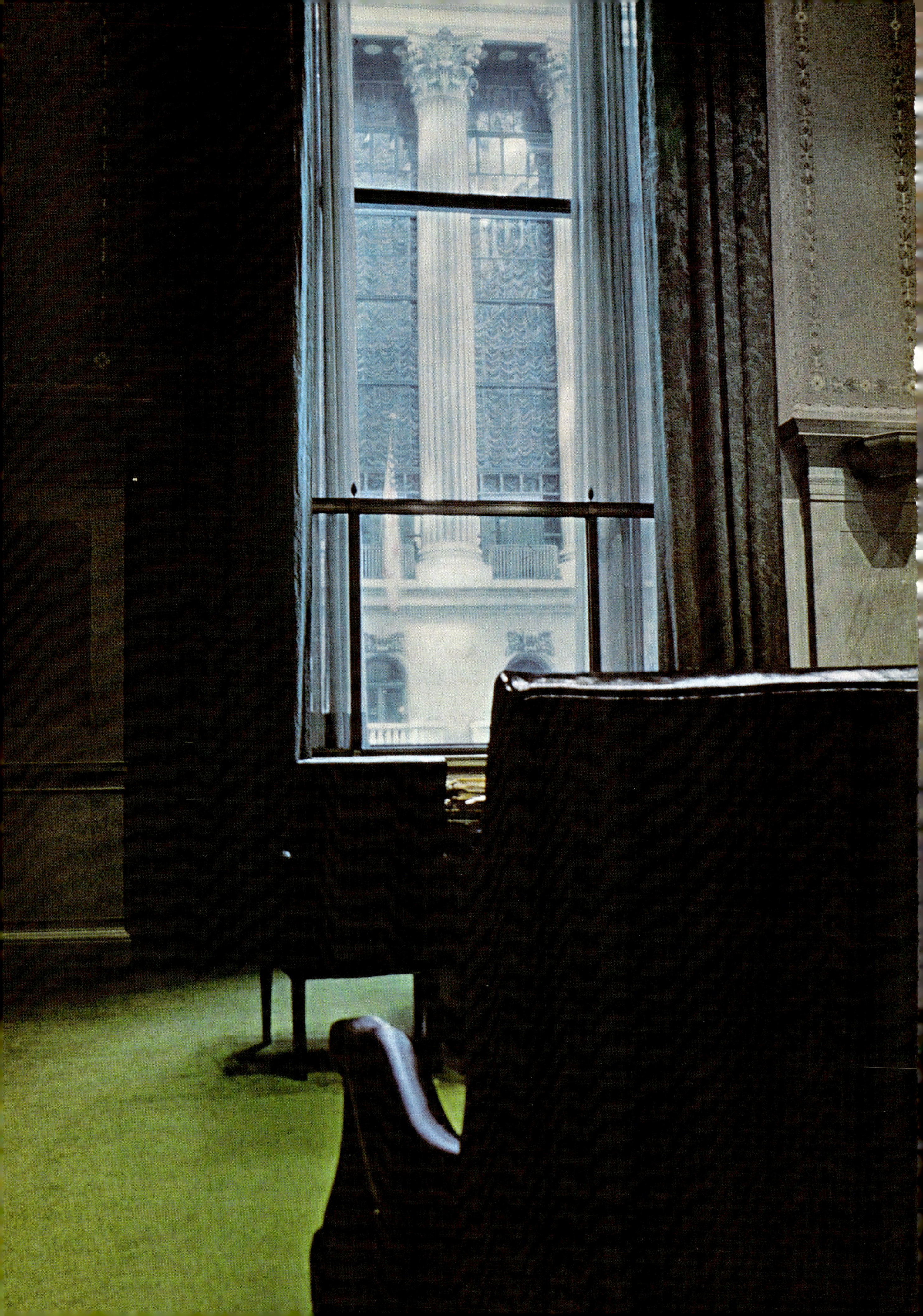

trolled by the firm. Not all their ventures, however, turned out triumphantly. A merger that brought together several major transatlantic steamship lines was a financial failure. A persistent pouring of money into an overbuilt New York, New Haven & Hartford Railroad brought disappointing results. An attempt to devise a plan for financing the London subway system was unsuccessful.

TRUSTS AND TRADE

Meanwhile, Guaranty Trust Company had pushed aggressively into the international field while also building at home a substantial clientele for its fiduciary services—acting as trustee for many of the new family fortunes that were coming into being in the bustling, growing, turn-of-the-century United States. Guaranty placed a representative in London in 1892 and opened a banking office there in 1897, the first overseas branch of an American bank. Later it established branches in Paris and Brussels. Its office in the latter city, opened in 1919, was for many years the only branch of an American bank there. In all three cities, Morgan Guaranty's branches today hold special rank by virtue of being so long on the scene.

Guaranty put a branch in Manila in 1901, followed by agencies in Hong Kong and Shanghai—forerunners of Morgan Guaranty's present active role in the Far East (today the bank has a representative office in Tokyo). Guaranty was the first American bank to develop important business in the Middle East. For a while, beginning in 1920, it had an office in Constantinople. (Early in 1965 Morgan Guaranty will open a representative office in Beirut.) Throughout the world Guaranty acquired a reputation for technical expertness in the financing of trade. It built up a global network of correspondent banking connections that included leading institutions in every commercial center.

In New York, Guaranty's growth was hastened by a series of mergers during the period 1910-12. Morton Trust Company, Fifth Avenue Trust Company, and Standard Trust Company were absorbed. The office of Fifth Avenue Trust, at 43rd Street, became Guaranty's first midtown branch. Today, quartered in a new building one block north of the old location, it is the largest of Morgan Guaranty's three midtown offices.

From a window on the main floor, a view of the columned front of the New York Stock Exchange, just across Broad Street.

WARTIME PARALLELS

During the years of World War I, the courses steered by the Morgan firm and by Guaranty drew into closer parallel. Both turned primary attention to public finance, at first raising loans in the U. S. market for the European governments that were buying supplies here, and later—after the United States had entered the war—helping finance this country's participation by buying and promoting the purchase of the successive issues of Liberty bonds. In addition, special roles fell to each of the two institutions as a result of its established leadership in certain fields.

Guaranty, for instance, had been for some time the most active American bank in the financing of cotton exports. When the outbreak of war in 1914 brought foreign sales of that commodity to a virtual halt because of credit uncertainties and shipping dangers, a Cotton Loan Fund totaling $135 million was mobilized to help growers and merchants avert a threatened market break. The newly created Federal Reserve Board headed the fund. Guaranty was a principal participant. The fund did its psychological job so quickly and effectively that few drawings on it occurred. As shipments resumed after the sudden paralysis, the financing of English and French cotton purchases attained such volume that Guaranty had to establish offices in Liverpool and Le Havre to provide the needed follow-through.

Guaranty's branch in London, a fixture of that city's financial district by the time war broke out, became a financial rescue station for American travelers who were stranded short of cash when British banks closed for four days immediately after the declaration of war. An emergency sub-branch was set up in the Savoy Hotel. It cashed checks, honored letters of credit, and did everything possible for people caught far from home by sudden events that stopped the normal financial machinery. Three years later, when Americans in uniform began pouring into France, Guaranty opened a branch in Paris to meet both their official and their personal banking needs.

A long-established position in Europe also brought unique wartime assignments to J. P. Morgan & Co. The firm acted as commercial agent in the U. S. for the British and French governments until this country joined the war. In this capacity it placed contracts with American producers for weapons, ammunition, and a wide variety of other goods needed by the Allies. The orders thus placed totaled more than $3 billion. The New York firm's close relationships with Morgan Grenfell & Co. in London and with Morgan Harjes & Co. in Paris provided the constant transatlantic liaison which was essential for this operation. These connections also smoothed negotiations for the underwriting of large British and French loans—in total nearly $1½ billion —placed with investors in the U. S. market.

The U. S. government was kept informed of these activities on behalf of foreign countries. When Congress voted this country's entry into the war in 1917, both purchasing and financing functions for the Allies were taken over by Washington. After the war, with the knowledge and often the encouragement of the U. S. authorities, who were anxious to promote European reconstruction and recovery, the Morgan firm managed the sale in the U. S. of bond issues

Receiving and paying tellers have their stations at a curved counter on the ground floor.

Overleaf: a view around the corner. The camera's circular sweep looks straight up at the entrance of 23 Wall. Then, in counterclockwise order, it takes in the New York Stock Exchange, Bankers Trust Company, Federal Hall Memorial, The Seamen's Bank for Savings.

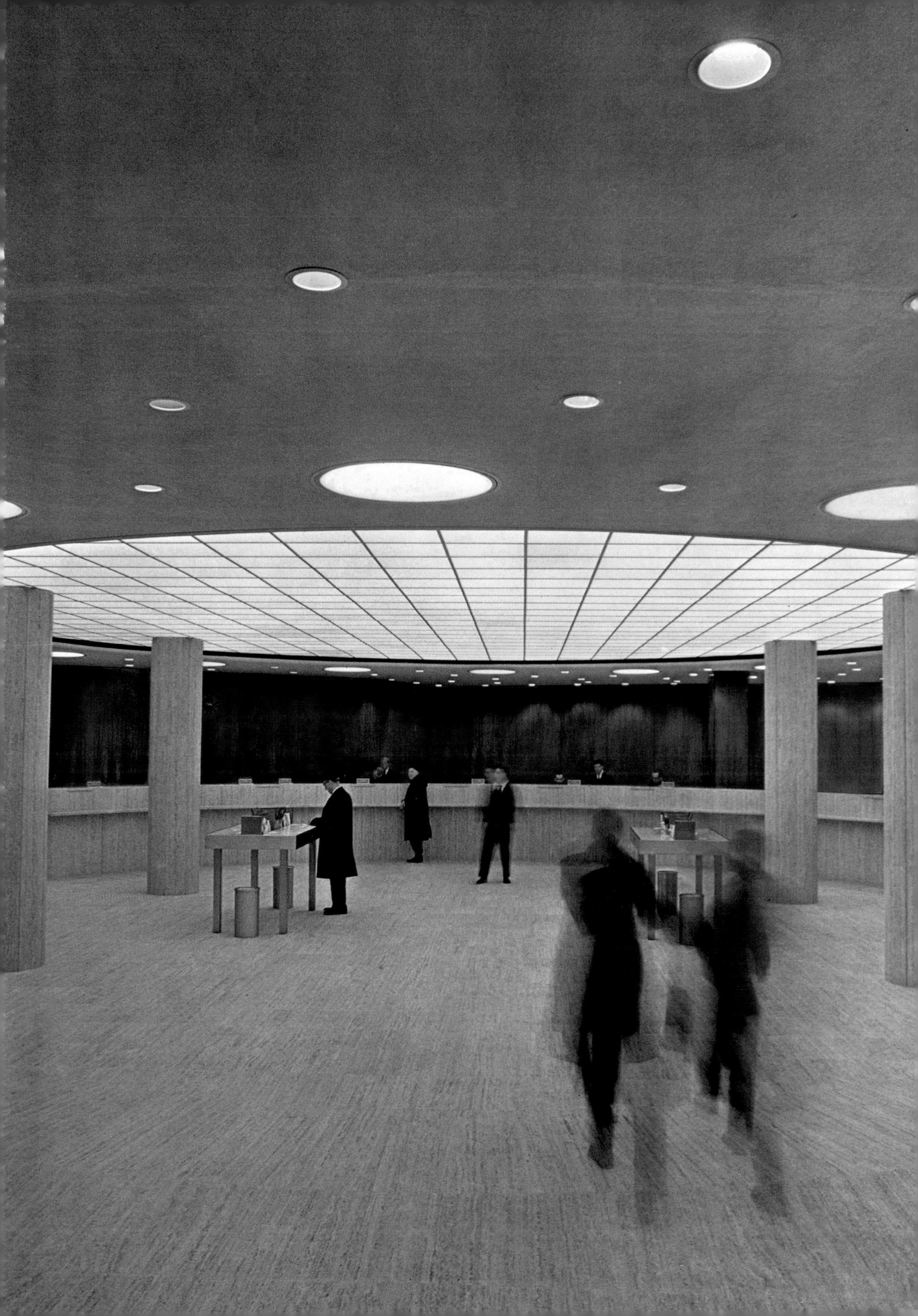

23

23

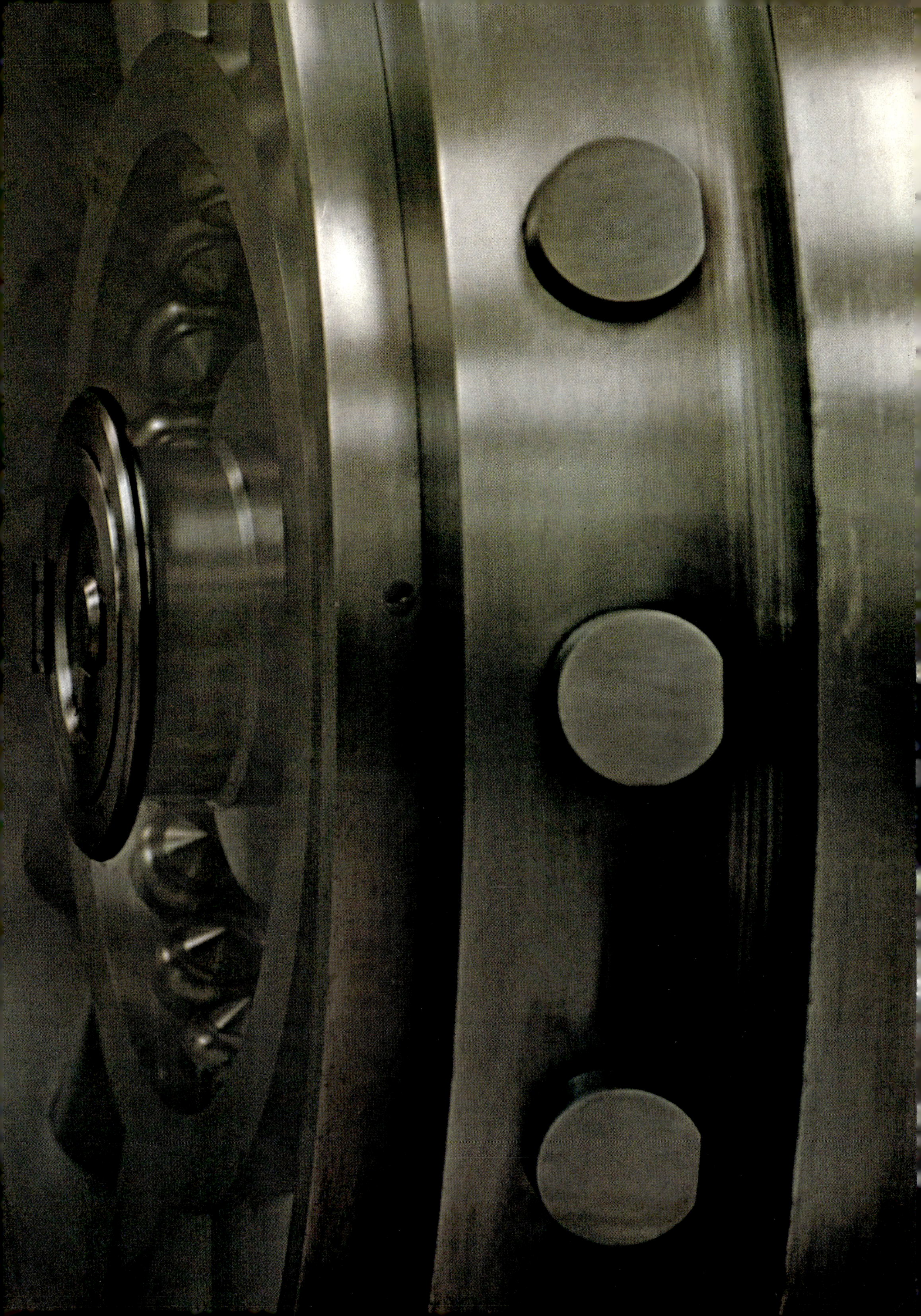

for a number of foreign governments and private companies. Its main activity, however, was the underwriting of securities issued by America's growing industrial and commercial enterprises.

STRETCHING TOO FAR

There was a strong resurgence of international trade in the early aftermath of the war. Markets around the world were hungry for goods after the long years of conflict, and an American economy that had expanded to meet the wartime need for production hastened to fulfill the pent-up demand. Guaranty, already a strong force in world-wide banking, moved aggressively into the financing of American exporters and foreign importers. It led a group of U. S. institutions in organizing the Mercantile Bank of the Americas to specialize in Latin American business. It also took a substantial interest in an Asian banking enterprise. And its own portfolio of advances on overseas sales of American goods grew rapidly.

Suddenly, in the fall of 1921, the trade boom suffered a severe setback. It had gone too far, too fast. Overseas buyers had inflated their orders to be sure of getting merchandise. Lenders had extended credit freely in the quest for business. All at once, the channels of trade were found to be choked with goods beyond the capacity of buyers to take or pay. Orders were canceled, shipments were refused, and there was a wave of defaults on trade credit. Guaranty, as a leader in this field, had its share of the large losses that were sustained. Its ownership of a one-half interest in the Mercantile Bank proved particularly costly. The Mercantile had lent heavily on sugar, and a sharp fall in prices had made many of the loans worthless.

A group of New York banks, sensing the danger of a generalized credit collapse, advanced funds to enable the Mercantile to go through liquidation in an orderly fashion. J. P. Morgan & Co. was prominent in the group. Thomas W. Lamont, a partner in the Morgan firm, was chairman of Guaranty's executive committee and had been on its board of directors since 1910. Another Morgan partner, George Whitney, became a Guaranty director in 1921. He and Mr. Lamont continued as directors until 1940, when J. P. Morgan & Co. changed from a partnership to an incorporated bank and trust company.

Personal ties among the three principal companies whose histories eventually would combine in Morgan Guaranty Trust Company had begun much earlier. In 1875 J. Pierpont Morgan was elected a director of National Bank of Commerce. He remained on the board until 1910. From 1893 until 1904, he was Commerce's vice president. At that time the bank had only one officer with that title, and the position did not involve day-to-day duties; on at least one

This vault door was installed when the 23 Wall Street building was erected in 1914. Its 52 tons of steel are so precisely balanced on the hinges that the door can be swung open or shut by the force of a single hand.

occasion it did entail, however, authentication of notes issued by the bank, and a few Commerce notes signed by Pierpont Morgan exist today in private collections.

J. P. Morgan, Jr., succeeded his father as a director of National Bank of Commerce in 1910 and served four years. Another Morgan partner, H. P. Davison, was elected to the board at the same time and continued on it until 1914. Mr. Davison was also on the Guaranty board from 1909 to 1914.

COMING BACK STRONG

Guaranty pulled through the trade collapse of 1921. At the year-end, capital funds showed a decline of $20 million—an indication of the severity of the losses. With all commitments honored and its credit untarnished, however, the bank made a rapid recovery and steadily built its share in the flourishing commercial banking business of the mid-1920's. Through its subsidiary Guaranty Company, it also carved an important niche in investment banking, underwriting issues of bonds and stocks and marketing them through a network of sales offices across the country.

Meanwhile, the activity reflected in the name the bank had assumed back in 1896—the care of other people's fortunes as trustee—continued to grow. The merger with National Bank of Commerce in 1929, creating a bank almost twice as big as Guaranty had been, capped the years of progress that followed the setback of 1921. It also produced an institution with capital funds greater than those of any other bank in the United States. This tradition of capital strength persists today in Morgan Guaranty's ratio of capital funds to deposits, which is one of the highest to be found among major U. S. banks.

More immediately in the aftermath of the Guaranty-Commerce merger, the combined bank's massive capital was to be a welcome bulwark against the tide of depression that engulfed the country and the world. Business volume and earnings shrank, as they did for virtually all enterprises, but the bank's soundness was never in question. It reopened promptly after the closing of all banks by official decree in March 1933. By 1936 it had recouped the decline in business volume and gone on to reach a new high level in total resources.

For the Morgan bank, the events of the 1930's introduced a fundamental transition. The Banking Act of 1933 required the firm to choose between the securities underwriting which traditionally had been the main thrust of its activity, and the commercial banking which it had been conducting in substantial volume but for a relatively small number of clients. On the premise that a strong investment-banking orientation would be a unique advantage in a commercial bank primarily serving business customers, the firm elected the latter option. Then, in the chilly atmosphere of

The main banking area connects 23 Wall Street (foreground) with large room and mezzanine in the 15 Broad Street building.

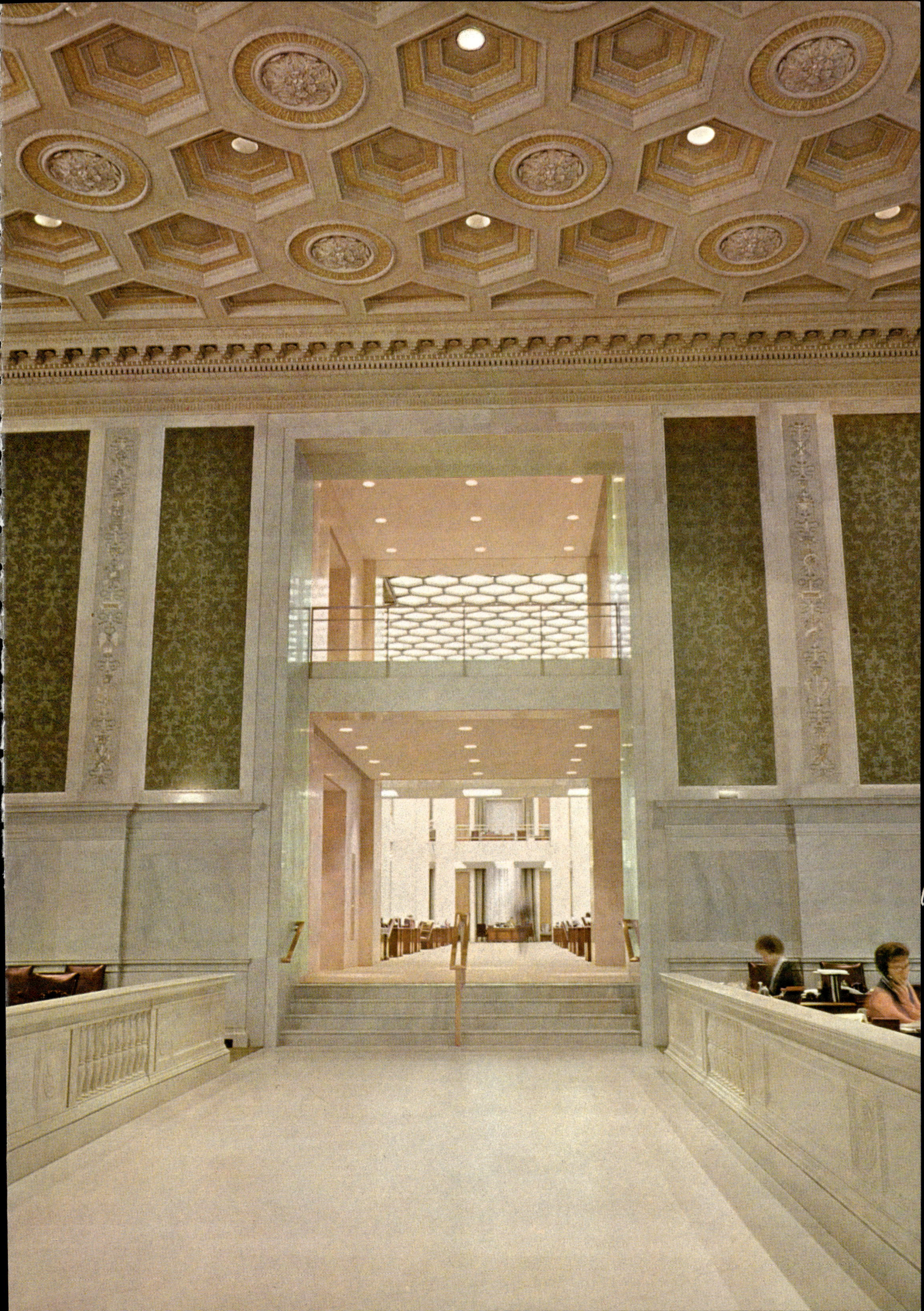

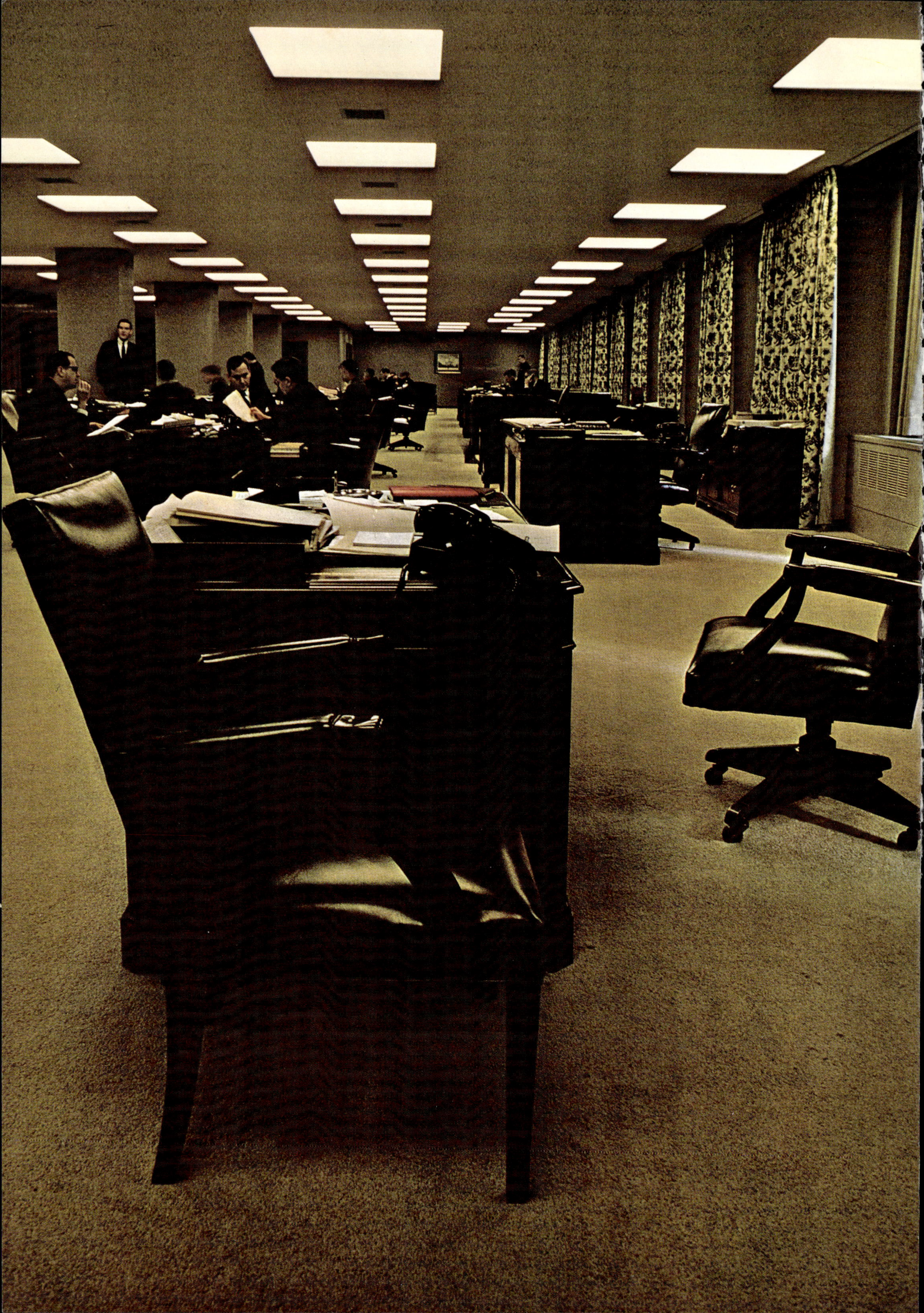

lingering economic depression, it set about broadening its base of services and clients.

As an integral part of the loan and deposit business that is the core of commercial banking, the firm continued the Morgan tradition of full and frank advice to clients on all kinds of financial matters. In the more prosaic areas of finance, it performed "agency" services—stock transfer, dividend and coupon payment, share registration—for some of the leading industrial corporations. It held seats on the principal stock exchanges. So long as it remained a private banking partnership, it was not authorized to act as a trustee. When it became an incorporated bank and trust company in 1940, it moved at once into the fiduciary field. This soon developed into an important part of the bank's business. It was one in which experience brought over from the investment banking days of the partnership proved especially valuable.

A NEW CHAPTER As both banks grew in size and scope during the lively years of business expansion following World War II, many of the commercial and industrial companies that they served were growing even faster. To keep up with their customers' needs, banks required not only larger accumulations of dollars but also new human resources of skill and talent, new depth of financial expertness, more extensive facilities at home and abroad. For many banks, especially in the largest centers, internal growth didn't come fast enough to insure that they could continue to match capabilities to their clients' requirements.

Morgan and Guaranty met this situation by combining their resources. Their merger, in 1959, solved the problem of size without diluting the specialization which had set them both apart from other major New York banks. But it created a problem of physical location. Neither Guaranty's main office, in the group of buildings centered around 140 Broadway, nor the space occupied by Morgan at 23 Wall and in the adjoining 15 Broad Street building would house the entire headquarters of the merged bank.

Out of sheer need for space, both locations were utilized while a plan was developed to bring the head office under one roof. The solution chosen was to occupy the entire 15 Broad Street building—which was owned by the bank but in large part rented to tenants—along with 23 Wall. A complete remaking of the interiors of both, to bring them together as a functional whole, began in the summer of 1961. The work was completed early in 1964. In its 50th year, the house on the corner where so much history already had been made was starting a new chapter.

Only a few any longer have first-hand recollection of the November day in 1914 when a new pair of doors marked

On the second floor, a section of the International Banking Division.

27

with the numerals 23 swung open on Wall Street for the first time. By the account of those who remember the first day of business in the new building, there was no ceremony, no speechmaking. Mainly there was irony in the absence of the man who had commissioned the structure and taken a large hand in shaping its design. Pierpont Morgan had died in the spring of the preceding year, while the new home for his firm was starting to rise on the corner he had known so long.

His mark was everywhere evident in the plans he did not live to see fulfilled. The architects, Trowbridge & Livingston, worked within directives he had set: the exterior would be of pink Tennessee marble, quarried from the same vein near Knoxville that had supplied the stone for Mr. Morgan's library on East 36th Street; the huge, five-sided banking room, some 15,000 square feet in area, was to be free of any column or other interior support. The latter requirement forced the invention of a system of overhead trusses, resting on steel carried up through the marble of the outside walls. The three upper floors and the great coffered ceiling of the banking room are hung from the trusses. Many architects at the time said the plan wouldn't work, but it did.

The cornerstone of the building, an unmarked block to the right of the main entrance, was laid on December 30, 1913. J. P. Morgan, Jr., who had succeeded his father as senior partner, troweled mortar to set the stone in place. In a copper box encased in the stone, he and his associates placed the usual memorabilia—a copy of the firm's articles of partnership, samples of the forms used for issuing travelers' letters of credit. They also enclosed a copy of the elder Morgan's will, a document remarkable for the tone set by its opening sentence—"I commit my soul into the hands of my Saviour . . ."—more than for the material goods it distributed. But Mr. Morgan's chief legacy to the enterprise he had founded was embodied in a paper that at the time may have seemed an odd memento to include among the sentimental contents of a cornerstone cache.

This was a transcript of the testimony he had given, in the last year of his life, before a Congressional committee investigating allegations that a "money trust" was controlling the access of American business firms to the capital and credit they needed. It was a hostile committee, and the questioning was harsh and prolonged. In the near aftermath of the event, it was hardly an episode to be remembered fondly. The passage of time, however, has confirmed the judgment of those who selected the text of the Pujo Committee hearings as a summing-up of Pierpont Morgan's career in finance. A quotation from his dialogue with the committee counsel probably has been cited oftener than any other statement he ever made as revealing his code of business and of life. Asked whether commercial credit was not

Movements in the money market are flashed instantly by an electronic quotation board in the government bond trading room.

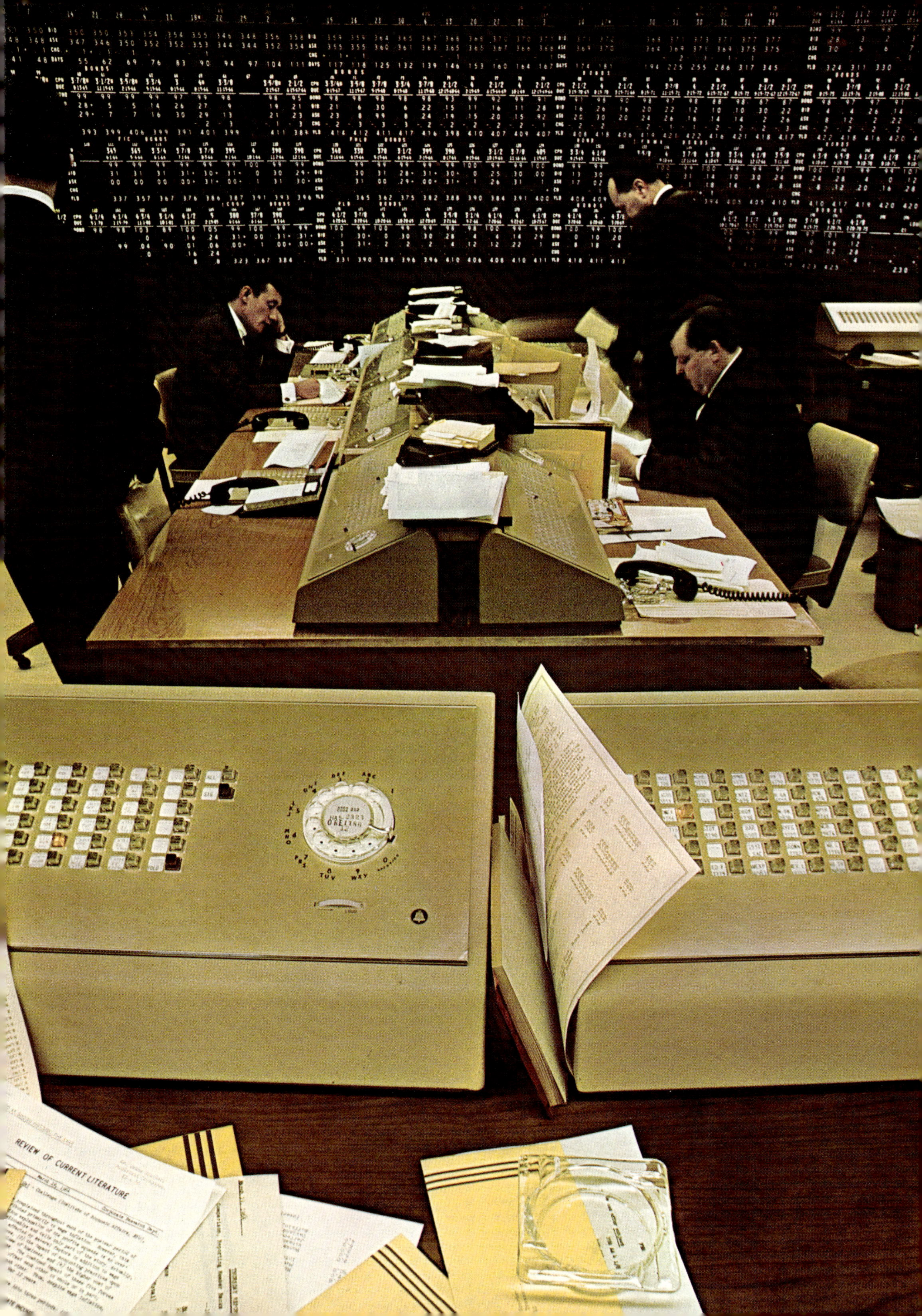
REVIEW OF CURRENT LITERATURE

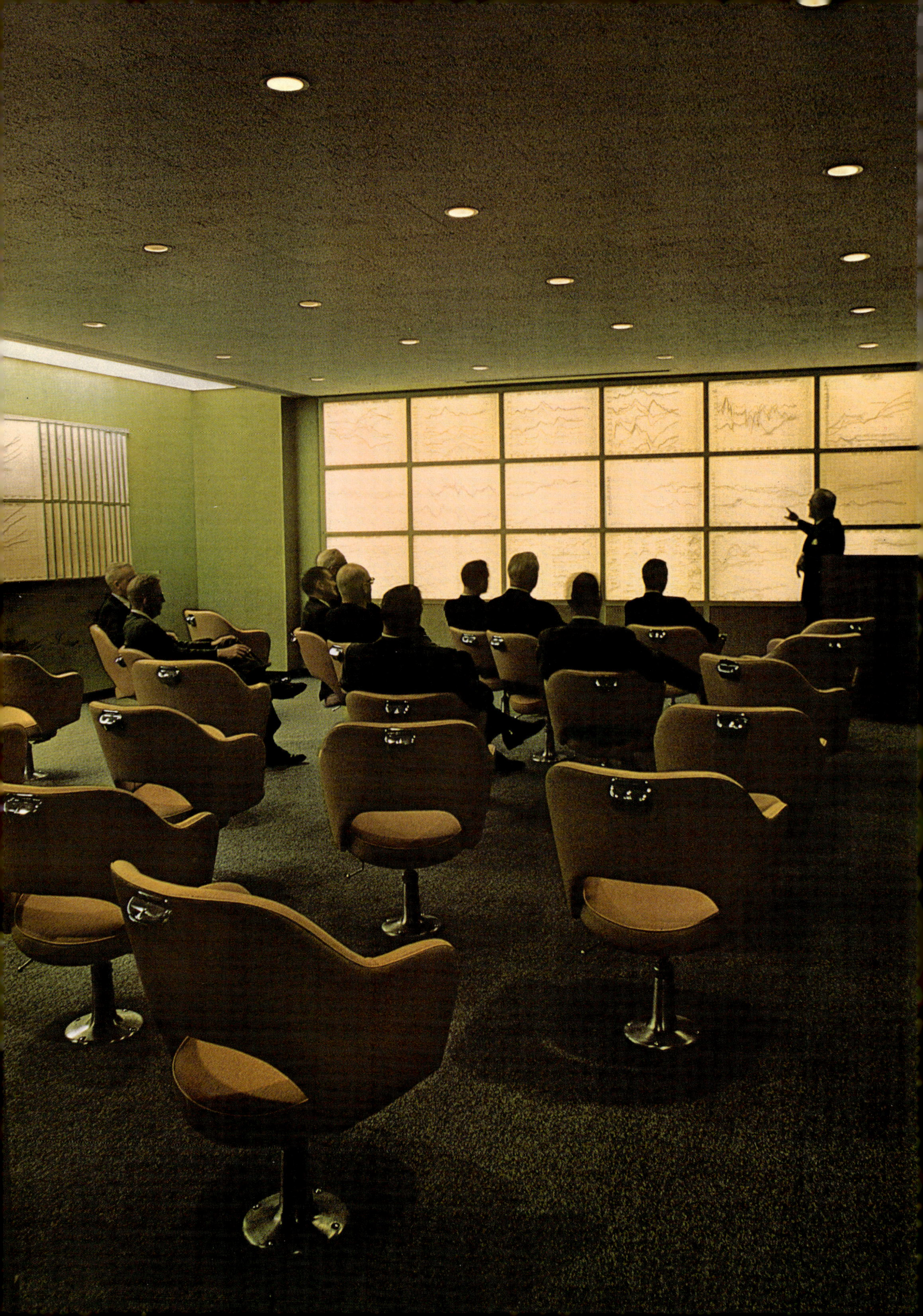

based primarily upon money or property, he said: "No, sir; the first thing is character."

To this the committee counsel, Samuel Untermyer, rejoined: "Before money or property?"

Mr. Morgan insisted: "Before money or anything else. Money can not buy it.... Because a man I do not trust could not get money from me on all the bonds in Christendom."

THE OLD AND THE NEW

On the outside, 23 Wall is little changed today from its appearance fifty years ago. The stout marble blocks on the north side show gouges dug by shrapnel hurled in the mysterious Wall Street explosion of 1920. Basement windows on the Broad Street side have been filled in with matching stone behind the original grillwork. Otherwise, all is as it was. The foundations as originally installed could support a building of some thirty stories above the four that stand, and the possibility of adding height received serious consideration when Morgan Guaranty was planning its present headquarters. No addition that architects could propose, however, would have preserved the building's character or its harmony with the historic surroundings. Tradition and aesthetics won the decision against enlargement.

The same considerations explain the continued omission from the main entrance of any identification other than the numerals of the street address. By the memory of persons familiar with the circumstances of the building's construction, the absence of a nameplate or other sign began as a coincidence. Supposedly, Mr. Morgan had specified that the tall marble columns on either side of the entrance be left bare because he had in mind decorative elements to be placed on pedestals in front of them. He died without having settled the matter with the architects, and his successors chose to leave the front unadorned—even though the firm name had been cut large in stone on the face of its earlier building on the same site. Because of the limitations within which it was designed, the entrance does not lend itself to the harmonious addition of an identifying sign. Meanwhile, the plain front itself has become a kind of identification.

Inside, the house on the corner keeps much of its original look, but there have been changes. The differences are most apparent in the main room, where officers of the General Banking Division confer with clients from every line of industry, trade, and finance. New warmth and texture are imparted by large panels of rich green tapestry, covering sections of the walls that formerly were mosaics of tiny tiles. Low marble balustrades, in place of the original screens of marble and bronze, give added openness to the large area unbroken by supporting columns. The sense of space is further enhanced by continuation of the banking room

In the chart room, data and analyses prepared by the bank's economists help clients make business and financial plans. Economic briefings for the bank's officers also are held here.

through a broad arch to the connecting floor and mezzanine of the 15 Broad Street building.

The most striking new feature of the banking room is a massive chandelier in the style of Louis XV. More than 1,900 pieces of crystal play and replay the brilliance of 220 individual lamps. Most of the pieces are from a collection brought to the United States from Austria-Hungary before World War I. The fixture weighs about two tons. It can be lowered or raised—at a speed of one foot per minute—by a power winch mounted on an upper floor.

Amid change, much in the main room remains as it was. The original fireplace stands in the south wall, near Broad Street. Above it is the Baca-Flor portrait of Pierpont Morgan, painted in 1911 and installed when the building was first furnished. Between the tapestry panels on the walls, and between the enormous windows, the narrow arabesques of mosaic still trace their symbolism of man's industrial and commercial pursuits.

When money moves, so do papers. Orders to transfer funds travel quickly to the proper desk.

TRADITION AND CHANGE

In this setting, compounded of tradition and change, a bank well into the second century of its life conducts today's business and prepares for tomorrow's. It is a business more varied, more complex, and more specialized than was known to any of the predecessor institutions. At its core are the historic banking functions—care of deposits, extension of credit, informed counsel on all kinds of financial questions. These are the concerns chiefly of the General Banking Division and the International Banking Division, whose more than 200 officers are based at the main office, three offices in midtown Manhattan, and seven offices overseas. At their desks and in travel around the country and the world, these bankers confer with clients to learn their needs and adapt the bank's facilities to meet them.

The facilities go far beyond the basic banking functions. They include, for instance, research that studies both the long-term trends of entire national economies and the performance of thousands of individual companies. More than fifty industry specialists in the Corporate Research Department maintain a continuing profile of every branch of business. Their analysis provides the basis for counsel to the bank's clients; they also undertake specific assignments for clients in connection with long-range financial policies, diversification plans, mergers and acquisitions.

Morgan Guaranty's heavy commitment to economic and financial research grows out of its concentration on serving the needs of business. It also is related to the bank's leading position in the management of trust funds and the furnishing of professional investment advice to individuals and institutions. The Trusts and Investments Division has the care of many billions of dollars in personal trusts, estates,

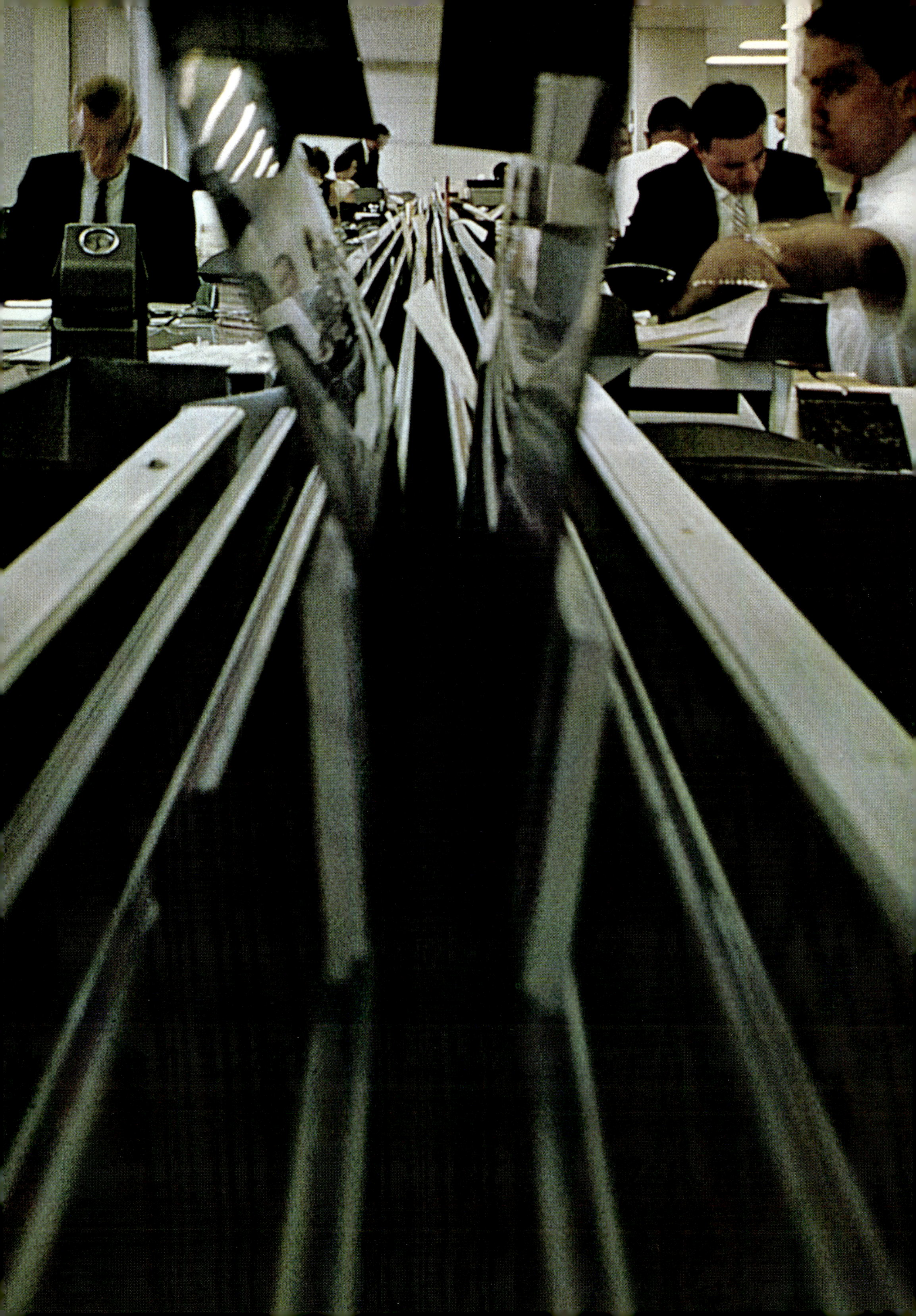

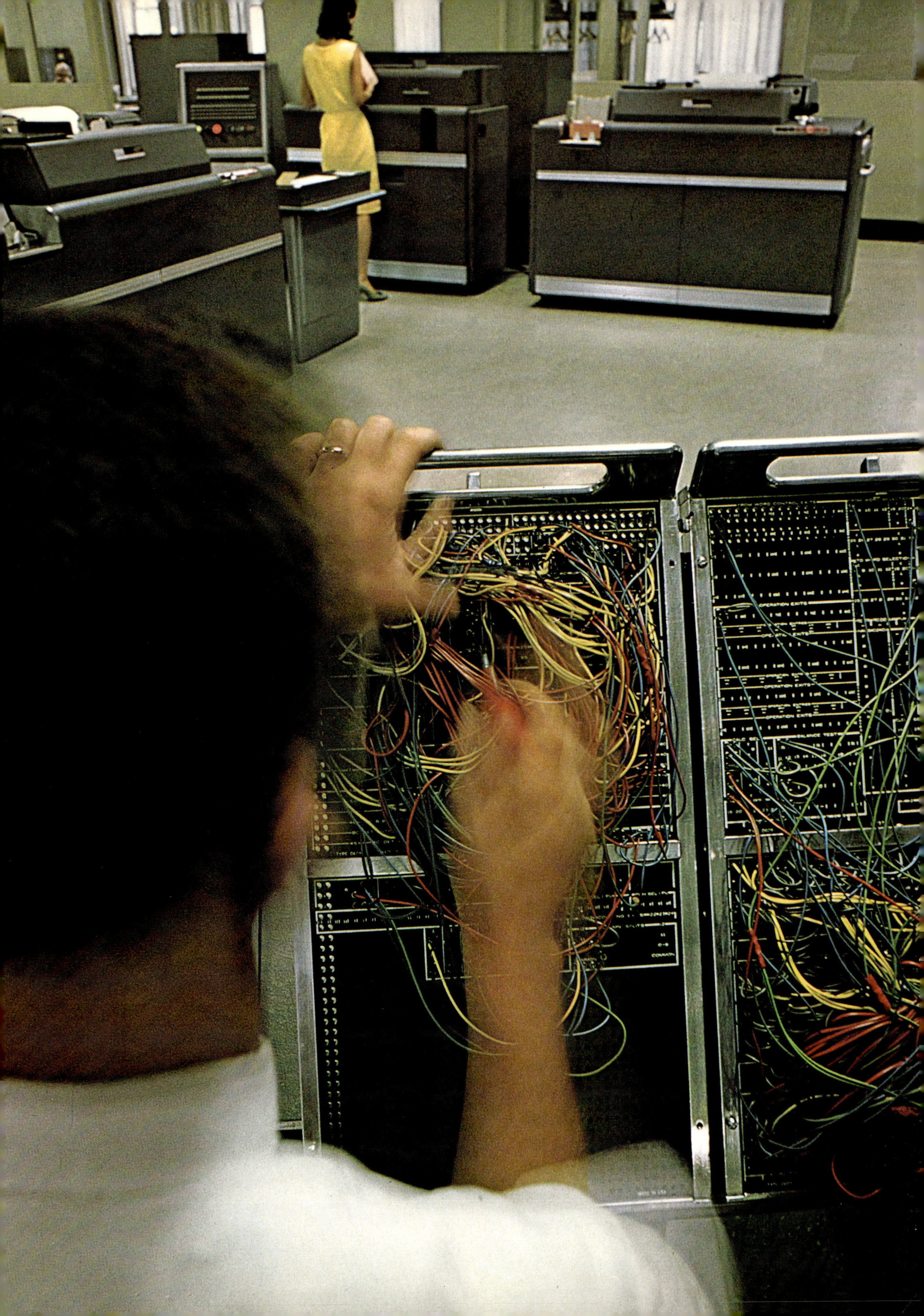
OPERATION EXITS
COMMON

pension and profit-sharing funds. It provides guidance to foundations, endowments, schools, philanthropic organizations, and individuals on the management of their investments. In this work it utilizes not only the experience and judgment of the senior officers and directors who make up the Committee on Trust Matters but also the steady flow of information and interpretation from the specialists in the Corporate Research Department.

THE MARKET FOR MONEY

Money, the business of all banks, is the business of Morgan Guaranty in a particular way. Serving as the medium of exchange in all markets, money also has its own market, and the bank at 23 Wall Street is at the hub of that swirling, sophisticated interplay of short-term funds known as "the money market." As a dealer in government securities, it buys and sells the obligations of the U. S. Treasury in larger volume than any other bank. It is a major force in the marketing of the issues of Federal agencies such as the Land Banks, Home Loan Banks, and the Federal National Mortgage Association. Acting as agent for its customers, it is the principal bank purchaser of commercial paper—the promissory notes by which finance companies and others borrow millions for periods ranging from three days to nine months. It underwrites and deals in the debt of states, cities, and other public agencies that borrow to build schools, lay sewers, clear slums, build housing, and provide a host of other kinds of public services.

It trades daily with banks all over the country in the esoteric medium known as "Federal funds"—the balances which banks keep at the Federal Reserve Banks. These constitute the only truly "instant" means of transferring cash from one city to another, because they can be switched from one bank's account to another's at the flash of an electronic impulse. Morgan Guaranty's predecessor, J. P. Morgan & Co., led the development of the modern Federal funds market, beginning in the early 1950's. Today the market is a recognized adjunct to the nation's central banking system, permitting a much more efficient use of reserves than otherwise would be possible.

Morgan Guaranty is a prime mover in another branch of the money market which one of its predecessors was instrumental in developing in the United States. This is the means of financing called the banker's acceptance, a form of credit used primarily to ease the movement of goods in trade. The acceptance was a traditional instrument of credit in Europe, but was used hardly at all in the U. S. until the Federal Reserve Act of 1913 made specific provision for it. Guaranty responded quickly to the opportunity thus created and soon became the major factor in the U. S. acceptance market.

The market in money is international. Morgan Guar-

Wires deftly inserted in a control panel tell the machines what to do.

anty's foreign exchange desk trades in all the major currencies to accommodate clients doing business overseas. Its volume runs well over $10 billion in a normal year. It advises clients on management of their foreign funds and provides up-to-date information on currency and import-export regulations in more than 100 countries.

COME THE COMPUTERS

When the building at 23 Wall first opened its doors in 1914, the paperwork was relatively simple. The accounts were kept in enormous ledgers by clerks who dipped pen in inkwell and wrote in an elegant cursive hand. In contrast, preparation of Morgan Guaranty's new headquarters involved extensive special construction and wiring to accommodate electronic data processing equipment.

Tools and technology have gone through a series of revolutions in the past half-century, but painstaking attention to detail is still indispensable in banking service. Behind the bold, inventive concepts that may be embodied in a major financial undertaking, there often comes long and tedious follow-through requiring technical skill and an abiding passion for accuracy. To insure the smooth flow of clients' funds, keep records of the vast traffic in securities, and produce the needed stream of current information on all the bank's transactions—all this is work not only for the newest of machines but also for the most careful of people.

Proficiency of this kind has, among other things, helped make Morgan Guaranty the leading bank in the field of stock transfer and related services—functions it performs for hundreds of corporations. Nearly 800 employees carry on this work in a separate installation occupying ten floors of rented space at 30 West Broadway. In the course of a year they issue and mail more than 12 million dividend checks to stockholders of client companies.

NEW ROUTES ABROAD

The history of 23 Wall—and of the banks which joined to form the institution now headquartered there—is closely bound up with international finance. The sweep of its interest today reaches farther abroad then ever before, and in new ways. In response to the surge of involvement in foreign business by American companies, Morgan Guaranty in recent years has added importantly to its already considerable overseas resources. It has established representative offices in Frankfurt, Rome, and Tokyo (and is about to open one in Beirut) to augment its banking offices in London, Paris, and Brussels. During 1965 a banking office with the full range of services will replace the representative office in Frankfurt, and another is planned in Antwerp, where Guaranty Trust had a branch from 1921 to 1940. Morgan Guaranty also has formed—under authority granted by a law called the "Edge Act"—two subsidiary companies with a wide scope of international activity. These are Morgan

The face of the computer reflects complexity and competence.

MORGAN GUARANTY TRUST COMPANY
OF NEW YORK

The 15 Broad Street lobby affords direct access to the higher floors of Morgan Guaranty's headquarters. The interior of the 38-story structure, which adjoins 23 Wall on two sides, has been completely rebuilt for use by the bank.

Guaranty International Banking Corporation and Morgan Guaranty International Finance Corporation.

Through these companies Morgan Guaranty has purchased minority interests in carefully chosen financial institutions in more than twenty countries. These include commercial banks, investment banking houses, and development banks designed to promote the growth of local industries. For Morgan Guaranty clients with overseas operations, the bank's connection with these institutions provides a special entree to prime local sources of finance and other helpful facilities. The services thus available to them—including medium-term and long-term credit and even securities underwriting—are far broader in most cases than could be provided by a foreign branch of an American bank.

In Paris, the overseas subsidiaries of American companies have access to the full range of investment banking services through Morgan & Cie S.A., in which Morgan Guaranty International Finance Corporation holds a 70% interest. In London, Morgan Guaranty's associate—Morgan Grenfell & Co. Ltd.—provides underwriting and other investment banking facilities. In the Netherlands, Morgan Guaranty recently has reinforced long-standing ties with the leading financial houses of Hope & Co., in Amsterdam, and R. Mees & Zoonen, in Rotterdam. Morgan Guaranty, through a subsidiary, has a minority share in the business of the two Dutch houses, and they in turn hold—as does Morgan Grenfell—a minority interest in Morgan & Cie.

AT THE HEART OF IT ALL   The widening range and diversity of Morgan Guaranty's operations overseas are closely related to the ascendancy of New York as a world financial center. In this rise the peculiarly efficient organization of the New York financial community has played a part. Not least among its advantages are those of physical location. In 1959, when the decision was made to keep the main office of the newly formed Morgan Guaranty in downtown Manhattan, Board Chairman Henry C. Alexander commented:

"We have concluded that the bank can best serve both its domestic and its international clients from headquarters located in the financial district. The concentration of financial activity in a compact, easily reached area offers many advantages both to the institutions located there and to their clients. It would be difficult, probably impossible, to duplicate elsewhere the convenient grouping of facilities which downtown Manhattan provides."

This is Wall Street, the busy cluster at one end of an island, where the world's greatest city began and where financial history never stops. At the heart of it all, the house on the corner at No. 23 looks forward eagerly to its role in the history that lies ahead.

Morgan Guaranty Trust Company
OF NEW YORK

23 Wall Street, New York, N. Y. 10015
HA 5-2323; Cable *Morgan*

Midtown Offices

Fifth Avenue at 44th Street, New York, N. Y. 10036
Madison Avenue at 60th Street, New York, N. Y. 10021
40 Rockefeller Plaza, New York, N. Y. 10020
MUrray Hill 2-1200; Cable *Morgan*

Offices Abroad

LONDON
33 Lombard Street, E. C. 3
MANsion House 7890
Cable *Garritus*

31 Berkeley Square, W. 1
MANsion House 7890
Cable *Guarmor*

PARIS
14, Place Vendôme
OPEra 24-20
Cable *Morganbank*

BRUSSELS
27, Avenue des Arts
Brussels 11.65.10
Cable *Morganbank*

FRANKFURT*
Zürich-Haus am Opernplatz
Frankfurt 727451
Cable *Morganrep*

ROME*
Via Parigi, 11
Rome 486706; 481488
Cable *Morganbank*

TOKYO*
Palace Building, No. 10
1—Chome, Marunouchi, Chiyoda-Ku
Tokyo 211-6761/3
Cable *Morganbank*

Representative Offices

Morgan Guaranty International Banking Corporation
Morgan Guaranty International Finance Corporation
23 Wall Street, New York, N. Y. 10015; HA 5-2323; Cable *Morgan*

Morgan & Cie S.A.
4, Place de la Concorde, Paris; 742-03-19; Cable *Morgancie*

Member, Federal Deposit Insurance Corporation

Printed in U.S.A.